Adult Coloring Books

Stress Relief Coloring Book
Featuring Sweary Words, Animals and Flowers

Rainbow Coloring

Follow us on Facebook: Rainbow Coloring Books
or add us on **Snapchat**: Rainbowcoloring
or just scan this picture using your snapchat account ☺

Get free pages to enjoy and color, bonuses, discounts and a behind the scenes look at our process.